CW00972763

First Published 2011 by Lulu Publishing

978-1-4475-2344-4

Pixie Kisses

Re-enchant your life, one act at a time...

Dedication

I dedicate this book to all those looking for a little bit of magic in their lives, to the Faeries who wish to guide us back to a healthy balance between work and play, and to My Faery Queen.

And I dedicate this book to all those in the world who feel lost and alone and without enchantment.

Acknowledgements

A heartfelt thanks goes out to the feylings on my mailing list, and to everyone who responded to the Pixie Kisses posted online.

Love to my friends and family who get excited for me as I follow this, admittedly windy, path, your encouragement keeps me going.

And to the sponsors of *The Faery Heart*, thank you!

Contents

Introduction

Do you ever feel like there is magic at the edge of your life, but it is easy to forget it? Do you find it easy to slip into a space where you miss the wonder waiting at the edges of your world, a space where you feel weighed down by the nine till five (or six till midnight!) of a workaday life?

Have you ever felt so sure that there is more than this to life?

Or have you found those sprinkles of pixie dust? The flashes of wonder? The kisses of the fey? *And do you want more?*

I know that each and every one of us could benefit from more playtime, more magic, more wonder. Every one of us is a little happier when our worlds are enchanted.

This book is here because we are right. There is more than the merely mundane world, more than the grey. There is more to life than this. Life is full of wonder and magic and pixie kisses. And sometimes it is dangerous too, and that is ok. Life is full, that is what makes it life.

Wonder at the light and the dark,

Feel the magic in your heart,

Break the grey world right apart,

And set the magic free!

Its time to re-enchant the world.

Do you want to get in touch with your Fae side? Or with the Fae themselves?

Do you want to bring Faeryland closer for yourselves, or for everyone?

Do you want to bring more magic and creativity into your life?

Do you want to face both the light and the dark and find wonder in both?

Or do you want all these things?

Whichever it is, the actions are the same, only the angle you look at the world changes. If you seek to know yourself, you'll understand the world better. If you fill your life with delight, others around you will also be delighted. We are each a part of this world, by choosing happiness for yourself, you choose happiness for everyone. In choosing magic and wonder in your own life, you re-enchant the world, one pixie kiss at a time…

This book was originally written as a series of blogposts and letters with the pursuit of enchantment in mind. As such you can dip in and out at random points for inspiration, or follow the thread from the entrance of the labyrinth along the path. Some kisses refer to suggestions made earlier in the series, at these points feel free to rifle back to those earlier moments, or experiment and see how you are inspired!

The Nature of Enchantment

To be Enchanted is...

To walk in wonder at the world, noticing the magic under the surface, aware of the shimmer of the connection of all life.

To see the unseeable, know the unknowable, hear the unhearable... when that which the limits of normality dictates we may not dwell upon is echoing in our hearts, we do not turn away.

To hold close those moments of delight, to hold them as precious. To honour wonder as sacred, and play as necessary.

To value love and beauty and joy, and to seek them out and share them at every opportunity.

To be connected and seek connection. To honour our Fae Selves, those parts of us that do not conform and love to play... and to honour the Fae, the spirits of the world who embody magic.

To wonder.

To delight.

To love.

To be so full of joy that it overflows and brightens our world, even if only for a moment.

Let the Pixies kiss you with delight and fill your life with enchantment, choose to be enchanted.

Pixie Kiss #1: Making Space for Enchantment

For something to enter your life, there must be space for it.

For enchantment to enter your life, you must make space to be enchanted.

So let's make space. Let's make our space enchanting. Let's provide a home in our hearts and our houses for the Fae to dance…

Even if all you can manage is a picture hanging on a wall, a postcard tucked in the corner of the bathroom mirror, a pendant, or a pocket-sized tin full of tiny pebbles and dried flowers, making an actual, physical place for enchantment tells your deep self, your subconscious, your child self, that this is something you want to give space to in your life.

Every time you notice it, you will remember.

Every time you give attention to it, the emotions and energies it invokes will ripple out into your life. Psychologically it will remind you of your dreams of an enchanted life. Magically, like attracts like, so you encourage wonder by depicting wonder. And, in a very real way, you are offering hospitality to those that would help you reach the state of enchantment.

If you want more faery magic in your life, make space for it, and they will come…

Enchant yourself.

Tips:

A small symbol is a place to start, a full-blown altar or faery garden is even more potent because the amount of time and energy you put into creating it echoes through your life. If you don't know how to begin, think of images that evoke enchantment in you, track some down. Find sculptures, toys, images and objects that remind you of the fae. Choose fabrics which you love to drape over a shelf, light candles in glass holders, burn incense that makes you think of wild places. Collect natural objects, leaves falling in the autumn, flowers gently picked, stones with patterns or holes… arrange these in a way that you enjoy! Coloured pebbles and sea-glass are lovely in pretty jars or a bowl, none of it has to be obvious to anyone else, this is just between you and the Fae. Mirrors and sparkly things are good too… and you'd do well to leave an offering for the Fae if you can.

*Use what feels right, those things that enchant **you** are what will work best. Make a beautiful space for enchantment in your life and see what happens!*

Playtime   9th December 2010

Hello Feylings!

How're you doing?

Its frosty where I am, and the cold makes the air so clear, so crisp it crunches as I walk through it. The ice crystals made delicate spiderwebs stand out in sharp focus against the dark green of a signpost they were draped on. I'd like to imagine the signpost said interesting things like:

This Way to Faeryland

Look Up for Dragons

and

Spin Three Times Sunwise to Fly

And then I wonder which way the spiders went...

I've been reading Havi Brook's blog[1] which is a little strange but utterly fantastic, about de-stuckifying; getting un-stuck in life. One post particularly made me smile, it is about treating everywhere in the world like a playground, specifically; a 'Jungle Gym'.[2] I remember loving these places when I was little, brightly coloured, full of places to climb and run and hide. Places to explore. So, this post, it talks about making everywhere a place to explore. Explore the space, play with whatever you find, and part of the game can be playing in a way that no-one else notices...

---

[1] www.fluentself.com

[2] www.fluentself.com/blog/stuff/jungle-gyms-everywhere/

It got me wondering... how can we live life like everywhere is Faeryland, like everywhere is magical, enchanted, sacred?

If I were a faery princess, or an enchantress, or a dragon, or... how would I choose my clothes in the morning? How would I walk? What would I eat? How would I treat the world around me?

How can I act today that makes me feel like a magical being? Because, if we are magical, then the world around us must be magical. And if the whole world is magical, then there is more space for enchantment and delight.

One thing I started doing this year was collecting pretty hair clips. I have a giant daisy, a peacock feather, and a rose on a hairband. When I wear these it's almost like wearing a crown, or a garland of flowers, and I feel like I've stepped out of a fairytale. I choose my shampoo based on how it smells, and how fun I find it, for example, I have bubblegum scented gel which makes me giggle and reminds me of Halloween. I'm also looking at my clothes more generally, having realised that how I present myself to the world has an effect on how others treat me, and how I feel about myself. I used to take the attitude of 'I don't care what people think', and I found this, for me, was actually defensive. Instead, now, I'm feeling my way around how I'd like to dress, how I'd like to present myself, how I can appear in such a way as to start the process of enchantment simply by being present. Dressing up in fairy wings has crossed my mind!

How about you?

With happy thoughts and pixie dust,

~Halo x

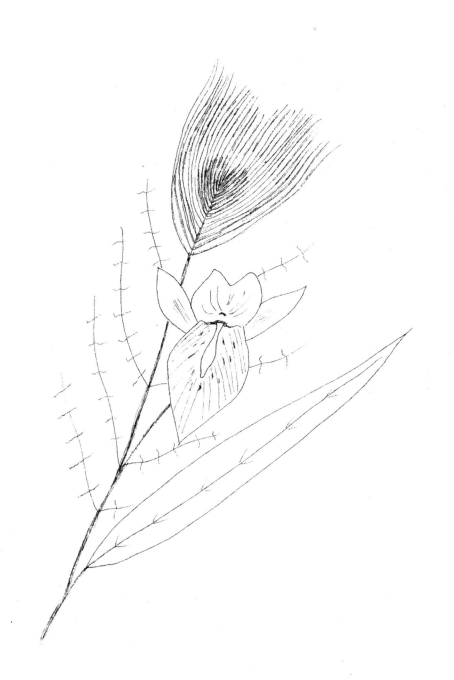

Pixie Kiss #2: Collecting Enchantment and Telling New Stories

Enchantment is, at its heart, en-'chant'-ment, a process which fills the world with chanting, i.e., new and beautiful songs which tell wonderfull stories.

Following the principle of magic that like attracts like, begin to fill your life with the kinds of wonder and stories of the magic that you choose to tap into.

Collect stories, poetry and art about the Fae, about enchantment, about wonder.

Surround yourself with beauty, with enchantment, and become enchanted. Share what you find with friends and enchant each other!

Then, take your favourite words – poems, songs, stories – out to somewhere beautiful and dedicate them to the Fae. Speak them aloud, with feeling, tell the stories to those beings you may not see but can feel nonetheless. They love a good story!

Telling stories is, in itself, a magical act. We live our lives through stories, absorbing images of the world, telling ourselves stories of ourselves and our world. We take on board the stories that the news tells us, that our friends repeat, that we learnt as children. We live our lives by these stories. And we can choose new stories for ourselves. Stories full of beauty and wonder and magic.

How many times do we say to ourselves…

I'm too…

I can't…

The world is horrible.

Life sucks.

Its too hard.

And so on? Sometimes it is true, for example; I am too big for size 8 jeans (or size 12 for that matter). As soon as this story becomes simply 'I'm too big' however, there is a problem. 'I'm too…' can lead to guilt, shame, disappointment, bitterness. All of these are unnecessary and unhelpful. My point here is not to go into important discussions about body image, but to illustrate how the stories we tell ourselves affect the way we think and feel. Plenty of people are able to help you if you're dealing with these kinds of harmful thought patterns, here we're going to choose to shift focus and create a new story for ourselves.

Collect enchantment, and begin to re-enchant yourself with words and pictures. Begin to literally choose the nature of the stories in your life...

Being Brave

13th December 2010

Dear Feylings!

The world has been so full of strange and scary things this past week or so. This is normal, it seems, and yet its been more obvious to me somehow just recently, with several friends out protesting against climate change, and tuition fee hikes in the UK, and Nuclear power. And then watching the clips of violence from the police, the anger and fear and hatred...

I got to thinking, in this way I am not brave. I cannot go and march the streets, risking kettling by police, violence from both sides, like my friends do.

But maybe, in other ways, I can be brave.

I dream of a world where there is more joy than sadness, more wonder and lightness of heart than fear and heaviness of the soul. I write, in the quiet of my home. I've begun to research the bad things I see, to question them, to try and get clear on why they happen, what they mean beyond the fact that they've upset people. Wikileaks and its ideals of freedom of information, the UK government renegading on promises. I arm myself with information and optimism, and I hope that I can help.

Can I live my life as an example of what I'd choose to see in the world?

Can my promotion of wonder, enchantment and joy really help?

Yes.

I have seen these things help people. I have seen that people follow the examples of others, I have seen that joy in one's life is contagious, and I have seen that wonder and magic in one's life can help one be a better person for oneself and others around us. Like a smile, enchantment is contagious.

Let us be brave and stand in our own lives, as the people we choose to be.

Let us be brave and make an example of ourselves, in the hopes that maybe someone will follow suit.

Let us be brave and not stay silent when things need to be shared, when love needs to be let loose in the world.

Let us be brave.

I am terrified of being seen as crazy, as silly, as dismissible.

And I choose to be brave. To do the work that only I can do in this way, alongside others doing the same thing, in their own way.

I am not the only one with this message, but I am the only me that can share it.

And you are the only you. You are the only one who can do what you can do.

Let enchantment fill your life and overflow. Let love and wonder pour through your heart. Let delight guide you.

Let us be brave as, together, we weave a web of enchantment through a world that needs it so much.

Let us wake up, and dream.

In Courage,

~Halo   x

Pixie Kiss #3: Understanding Enchantment

What does enchantment mean to you?

Look over the stories and pictures you've collected which delight you, and begin to get a sense of what enchantment feels like. If you have one, spend some time with your Altar to Enchantment, your Faery space, musing gently on what 'enchantment' means… ask the Fae that live on the edges of your consciousness to inspire you, even if you're not sure they're there yet…

You might want to write some notes, brainstorm, or draw, make collages or music or whatever helps you gather your thoughts into one place. When you have an idea of what enchantment means to you, see if you can express it somehow on a piece of paper that you can keep somewhere visible in the space you've dedicated to Faery – or somewhere you'll see it but others won't if you have people around who are less than supportive.

Next, begin to think about how that sense of enchantment might be expressed in your life.

If you were enchanted by life, what would that be like?

If life were enchanting, full of wonder and delight, how would you start each day? What would you wear? What would your home look like? How would you move through your day?

Once you have an idea of how you think that might look, take a deep breath and relax. Let your mind open to inspiration and ask yourself this:

What little thing can I do today to bring that feeling, that life of enchantment, into my day right now?

Write down any ideas that come to you, however silly, write them all down until you feel done. Then look them over and see which ones appeal to you today, and if there is one you can start right away.

Perhaps you'll choose to wear colours which make you feel like a Queen, or a Dryad, or an Enchanter. Perhaps you'll swap your shampoo for one which smells to you like faeryland and magic. Perhaps you'll choose to wear flowers in your hair each day, or to learn to dance, or to start a gratitude journal, or a dream diary. Perhaps you'll choose from now on to only buy beautiful things, or to leave gifts for strangers in bus shelters, or to move your desk so you can see out through the window while you work.

Choose something that works for you, and as that becomes habit, you can add another thing, and another. Begin to change your life. Choose the things that make you feel happy, and let that joy radiate out into the world.

For now, an understanding of what enchantment means to you, and an idea of how you'd like it to manifest in your life is what we're aiming for. Spend some time with yourself and your stories, at your altar or in a special place, and open up to a sense of enchantment. Once you know what it feels like, it becomes easier to invite it in…

Midwinter Respect

Merry Midwinter my lovelies!

A little solstice Haiku for you, in honour of all the snow and the faeries of the freezing...

> Cold kisses my nose.
> Jack Frost is dancing – carefree
> as snow slows our world.

I was thinking about Jack Frost as the train trundled through the countryside which bears his mark, and I realised that he illustrates a very important lesson for relating to Faery, and to Nature. The key to having positive dealings with these beings, who are not human, who embody the powers of the natural world (just as we, as part of the natural world, are Fae at heart, but that is for another time), is respect.

Respect their power.

Respect your limitations.

Respect their beauty.

Respect your abilities.

If we approach the Fae, and the snow, with respect for their powers which we do not control, and understand our own selves enough to go only as far as we are able to at that moment, then we can slow down and love them for their beauty, their otherness. And we can slow down and love ourselves for ourselves. And from respect, love grows in and for ourselves and between us and them.

Through love we realise that there is no us and them, only us, in relationship. We, human and non-human souls all, have gifts, strengths and limits. And we can connect, we can live together well if we approach each other with respect and love.

I hope you have a beautiful midwinter, and that the snow sparkles in the sun as the days begin to lengthen.

Happy thoughts and Pixie Dust,

~Halo x

Pixie Kiss #4: The Magic of Trees

From Thomas Moore's *Re-Enchantment of Everyday Life*:

"Every patch of ground that has a tree growing in it echoes Eden and is a reminder of our origins in an enchanted garden. Once we stop taking trees literally, we begin to see how they frame the world we look at every minute of our outdoor life... Eden is always with us, unless and until we narrow our vision, forgetting myth and disregarding aesthetic perception, and the trees of Eden are also always with us, full of mystery and implication."[3]

Trees are central, in so many ways, to our lives. We know that they provide oxygen, and soak up CO_2... we breathe *with* the plants of the world, we breathe out as they breathe in, they breathe out and we breathe in.

And trees are especially special, not only for their fruit and their wood, their shelter and their roots holding the earth together, but also for their presence. As Thomas Moore begins to say in the quote above, trees hold a special place in our mythologies, stories and hearts.

Midwinter is the time of year where many people decorate trees, or make Barbara Twigs, or burn Yule Logs, honouring trees even in our consumer-orientated lives. If we can do this mindfully, and not simply out of habit, then the act of choosing and decorating a tree can be enchanting... and the trees which sparkle with snow and fairy lights in the dark winter nights certainly enchant me! And decorative trees aren't restricted to Winter, either, there are Easter branches and Maypoles as well.

---

[3] Thomas Moore, *The Re-Enchantment of Everyday Life*, (HarperCollins Publishers, 1996)

The decorating of space for festivals, like Yule, Christmas, Halloween and even birthdays, is a way of bringing enchantment into our homes. We change the space to reflect the energy we choose to invite into our homes. Connecting with trees orientates us in the world, reminds us of the World Tree (present in most, if not all, cultures), and soothes our souls.

The hype of Christmas may be overwhelming, but the acts involved are all, in themselves, things we can take on board. Decorating our home with love and delight, connecting with trees, treating our time and space as time and space to celebrate in, all these are positive acts.

It is not just trees which we take too literally, our lives have drifted away from mythology, and it is the sense of layers, magic and wonder in a world with myth embedded in it that makes our hearts sing.

The many thoughts in this post, then, unravel into one shining question:

How can we reconnect with the magic in the world?

And a solution:

Remember that the whole world is ensouled, and allow ourselves to be enchanted by it. Start with trees, trees which span the worlds, trees which are so much more than mere building materials.

Dedicate each day to Enchantment

Imagine every day was a devotional act, for those of us dedicated to delight, however informally, this is what we strive for. Life is not all flowers, but beauty blossoms everywhere.

The simplest Pixie Kiss you will ever find is to dedicate each day, upon wakening, to enchantment. Start now.

Breathe deep.
Allow your heart to open to beauty.
Decide, today, that you will be open to enchantment, that you will cultivate an awareness of the wonder surrounding you in each moment.
And, when you forget, breathe and commit again.

Every moment is full of magic.

You choose how you see the world.

Make it magical!

Today, I choose enchantment,
Today I choose wonder,
I dedicate this day to delight.
I choose to follow enchantment where it leads in love and trust.

Pixie Kiss #5: A Faery Guide

Every journey is better with company, and this path is no different. Of course, the option of company from at least two realms is less familiar to our culture, but I'm sure we'll manage!

Who better to guide our efforts in bringing together the faery and human realms than a Fae who is doing this themselves? Here I present a simple exercise to reach out to one who would help. The philosophy of faery, my ideas behind what they are and what their relationship is to us I have detailed in my other book, but it is enough, for now, to be aware that there is more to this world than meets the eye. And, well, hooking up with someone who can guide you through the parts of their world and magic while you help them with ours can only help with bringing the realms closer.

So, to action!

Find somewhere quiet, safe, magical. It might be a quiet space outside, or it might be your Faery Altar. Your choice. Allow protection to enfold you, however you do this normally if you have a set way, or simply by imagining a sphere of light around you keeping you safe and asking for the blessing of the Faery Queen.

Relax and slow your breathing a little.

Count your breaths backwards, from 30 to 1, imagining each in-breath draws in light to feed you, and each out-breath releases tension. Allow yourself to relax.

Imagine you are surrounded by a green mist and you begin to float.

Float up and up, breathing softly, deeply, gently.

Hold the intention in your heart to meet a friendly fae, one who would like to team up with you on this journey of re-enchantment, one who chooses to be an ally.

Let your body and mind relax in the green mists of faery, and soon images and impressions will begin to come to you. Watch them, allowing the protection you called earlier to hold you safe. Watch them until one begins to solidify into an independent being, a fae who chooses to be an ally on this path.

Interact with them for a while, get a sense of who they are, and whether you are right for each other.

When you feel ready, bid them farewell and allow them to drift back into the mists... and feel yourself slowly floating down, back to earth, back to your self, your body.

Allow the protective sphere to dissipate if it feels right. Ground. Take notes. Eat something. Move around. Remember your new ally, they can help you navigate Faeryland, you can help them navigate the human realm. Together you can cross between worlds and bring enchantment closer...

You can repeat this as often as you like to meet them on other occasions, or, if no ally appeared at first, to seek again. Get to know each other, treat them with respect, and don't make any promises until you are very certain what you're promising!

Simple, and effective.

Choice, Fear and Limitations 7th January 2011

Hello Feylings!

I finally moved into my new home on New Year's Eve. It's very strange, having my own place (which I share with my bunny and my sweetheart), and realising that there is so much to be done! It's exciting, an adventure, and I'm mulling over how I can unpack and arrange my home in such a way as to invite in the kind of enchantment that I love.

At the same time, the Calendar year has begun, accompanied with a flurry of resolutions and intentions, goal setting and reviewing. It amuses me to realise that I've spent the past 6 months or so doing this, seeking clarity for which direction I would choose.

It's all about choice. Every moment.

This place, my new home, it came into my life when I chose to move back to Wales. I made a choice. Until that moment I'd oscillated between what I wanted, what I thought I should do, and being completely confused. As soon as I got clear, as soon as I chose, opportunity arose. The same with work. As soon as I stopped worrying and decided I was moving and that it would all be ok, an opportunity arose for me to keep my job and live back here. Once I knew what I wanted and said 'this', the world moved so I could have it.

The problem now is that some of what I asked for, some of the how, I dictated from a place of fear instead of trust.

The fear means its likely that I'm going to be stretched, limited, in ways I don't want to be.

Nevertheless, the fear is only trying to protect me, so I recognise it, and I'm working slowly on myself to let this fear not hold me back anymore.

When I make decisions and trust that the outcome will be good, it is. When I ask for something, it manifests. When I limit my asking, the manifestation is limited. Its strange how all those books on magic are right, you get what you ask for.

What I know, though, is that asking from a place of trust leads to enchantment. The very fact that the universe responds to what I request shows me that the universe is listening. The world is alive.

Trust, coupled with respect for yourself and your environment, is a key to enchantment.

Fear limits enchantment.

Choose, every day, to move towards the state you would prefer to act from. It helps to know who you are, what motivates you, what fears you carry, what enchants you. When you know yourself, you can see the patterns you act from. In myself I can see patterns of fear for survival (and inherited beliefs around the lack of value my chosen path has, but that's another story). Over time I've been able to move through these fears a little, enough that I'm now writing this, committed to enchantment, enough that now I can ask for what I want, even if sometimes I limit what I ask for! :)

What are your patterns? What are your fears? How are they protecting you? How are they holding you back? Understanding your limitations is the first step to releasing them. Stepping beyond the limits of a fearful life leads to enchantment.

Good luck!

 Happy thoughts and pixie dust,

~Halo x

Pixie Kiss #6: Knowing Your Heart

Who are you?

Who do you dream of being?

To be enchanted without becoming lost it is key to know your own heart, the centre of your self, the home of your soul. So now we turn from the space around us, and the beings that are our allies, and the enchantment already in the world, to face our own selves.

There are entire libraries on this subject, legacies, traditions and stories galore. My first book, The Faery Heart, is itself about getting to know your own self in the context of this path we are treading... and some of the foundational ideas which has guided me so far.

It is simple, in truth, and yet we are complicated creatures, layered within and without with stories and ideas and labels we don't always realise we hold, so I offer this very simple suggestion: take some time to explore what is in your heart right now.

Sit and breathe gently, use the meditative exercise I outlined in the fifth Pixie Kiss, breathing slowly and deeply, counting from 30 to 1, and allowing the green mists to rise and carry you gently. This time set your intention to see what is in your heart. Ask yourself the question: who am I?

Draw a heart shape on a piece of paper and begin to fill it with all the things you feel you hold in yourself right now. Qualities, labels, stories, images, feelings, desires...

When you are done, take a deep breath, and relax as you breath out.

Now begin to fill the space around the heart with those things you'd like to bring near yourself, closer to your heart.

And again, when you are done, breathe in deeply, and breathe out the tension and extra energy you are holding. Let yourself relax, and come back to awareness of where you are physically.

You can ask your ally to watch over you if you like.

Give yourself a break, ground, take notes if you need to. Leave the piece of paper in a safe place for at least an hour or two, then come back and look it over. See if anything surprises you or if there are patterns.

I'd encourage you to seek out other self-exploratory techniques, if you don't have some under your belt already, and to really begin to explore what is in your heart, who you are.

Some other things to ponder, without judgement if you can:

What does enchantment mean to me?

Why am I interested in bringing more of this into my life? Into the world?

What are my expectations around this path of enchantment?

Why am I drawn to the Fae?

What are my patterns of thought?

What are the connections between who I am, and how I would like to be? If they are different, what is stopping me from moving from one to the other, and why do I want to be other than I am?

On Grounding

The earth beneath your feet, where your bones rest, supporting your muscles...

As you reach towards the sky above...

When we walk the paths to Faery we drift a little from the world that is our home, and so we need to return again. Grounding is the process of coming home, of returning to our bodies, of touching down again.

We are made of the earth, which is formed of stardust, and so we belong on the earth but are drawn to the stars.

Remember, when you finish a trance, when you need to touchdown after flight, that you are a physical being in a material world, at least in part. Some good ways to ground yourself include;
Eating something starchy
Patting the edges of your body to remind yourself of your boundaries
Feel the land beneath you, the bones within you
Allow any excess energy you have to drain away into the earth
Say your own name aloud
Go and do something mundane

After flight, it is important to return to your body, your life, the earth. Find ways that make you feel normal again so you can act in the world of daily life.

Pixie Kiss #7: Moments of enchantment

A simple act can be the most powerful one.

When we open to enchantment, we open to magic.

As children we already knew what it meant to be enchanted, to find wonder in every moment, to see the world around us as alive. Because of this we could wish upon a star each night, and have our wishes come true, we had rituals of enchantment, and as adults we can foster these further, we can engage in awareness and gratitude.

Awareness and gratitude open us to enchantment, wonder, joy.

This Pixie Kiss is a reminder to dust off those rituals that we held dear as children... and we can also build new ones. Some of my favourite, gathered from other places over the years, involve journaling. I love to use intuitive collaging, based on Sheena Frost's Soulcollage process, or to ask myself questions like:

How did I feel today? What have I learned?

What have I achieved today, this week, this month? (A list of things I have done, instead of things to do, so I can see how far I have come and let go of guilt!)

What am I grateful for?

What do I love?

If I could do anything, what would it be? (Dreaming big! Then I look at what might be stopping me and I open to wondering about how to shift those things. Slowly, things change.)

What is the universe telling me?

Something you may choose, to bring some of the enchantment back into daily life, is to consciously reintroduce some of the acts which encouraged a playful, wonder-filled outlook. Think back over your childhood, what rituals did you have that might fit into your life now?

Perhaps you wished on the first star each evening, or left a mouthful of every drink for the faeries. Perhaps you had a rhyme for luck, or a lucky charm you carried with you.

These are not actions of superstition, but rituals you can enact on a daily basis, consciously, with the intention of bringing magic into your life. Choose the rituals which you feel focus on the wonderful in the world, and re-adopt them as daily spells for enchantment.

Let every moment have the potential to be enchanted, and use those tools of wonder that already live deep in your bones...

Light a candle and ask yourself about the good things in your life. Remind yourself of the enchantment already present in your world.

Tiny Things

Spread your wings out wide, m'dear,
Let them catch the sun.
Open your heart to life, sweetheart,
And let the beauty come.
Take a moment, every day,
To breathe in all delight.
Let your spirit overflow,
With all you feel tonight.
Notice all the little things,
The sweetest of them all,
Allow tiny joys to kiss your life
And into enchantment fall.

Pixie Kiss #8: Noticing Beauty and listening to Faery Music

This week, take your camera for a walk.

Pick a day when you have an hour or two to wander and go for a walk. In the Northern Hemisphere it is still cold this time of year, so respect the powers of Jack Frost and wrap up warm... and go out anyway.

Look around you.

Breathe in the beauty of the world.

Notice the little pieces of nature that peeks through the cracks in the pavement, or the majestic sweep of tall buildings, or the charming creepiness of abandoned buildings. Notice the expanse of sky above, or the crumbling stone beneath your feet. Notice the smells and sights and sounds, and take pictures. Really focus on the world around you.

Opening to the world opens you to the layers of magic in the world, the realms which lie just below sight, just below the obvious.

Open to beauty, open to noticing, open to wonder.

Use your camera to focus your self on the world... and open to the possibility of the Fey beings that surround you. The conscious blueprints of nature, the souls of the world.

If everything is a vibration, and vibration is sound, can you feel, in your bones, in your heart, the song of the Fey?

Invite your Faery guide to join you as you wander and wonder. Be open to their presence. See what happens.

Home

21st January

2011

Hello Feylings,

We've friends coming over tomorrow. The place we've moved into needs redecorating, the walls are filthy and cracked, everything is dirty, and the ceiling is orange with tar. Well, it was. My sweetheart and I have been cleaning, and while I was away working he and a friend cleaned and decorated the kitchen.

It strange how much this helped me settle. We've been here for a couple of weeks, but with so much to do I've not yet made the flat into a home yet.

And this is important. Home is important. We can go into the world and do great things, but if our roots aren't sunk deep into the ground, if we've not got a safe, nurturing place to return to, if we have no home, we have no anchor, there is no ground under our feet. We tire and have nowhere to rest.

When we venture out into the world, as we reach out to re-enchant the world around us, we have to remember to keep our home in order.

Home is important.

Home gives us a sense of safety, belonging, stability.

Home nurtures our souls.

Having a home, setting down roots, keeping the place we live in enchanting, all these things give us more energy to make changes elsewhere.

Before you go out on a Faery Adventure, before you listen to the music outside, take time to listen to your home. See if, perhaps, you need to make changes so that you feel safer, nourished, enchanted. And, if you don't already, leave an offering out for the spirits of the house... open up to the possibility of building a positive relationship with the house spirits. You do share the space, after all.

Applying the practice of listening to your home, as well as the outside world, will slowly reveal how your house is a home, and what may need to change to help this become more true. Happy home-making! I'm washing the living room next :)

Happy thoughts and Pixie Dust,

~Halo x

Pixie Kiss #9: An Enchanted Key

Inspired by Cat Valente's *Girl Who Circumnavigated Fairyland in a Ship of Her Own Making*[4] this kiss is about keys.

Keys are important. With keys we lock secrets away in private journals, we open doors, we mark a rite of passage in which we receive the ability to choose when we enter and leave our own homes. Locking and unlocking, closing and opening, protecting and revealing... keys mean so much.

Keys are symbolic, and real.

What doors are open to you?

What doors are closed?

What doors do you hold the key to, but have not yet unlocked?

Find an old key and decorate it. Use coloured wire or thread or ribbon. Use paint or clay or beads. Use whatever comes to hand, or special materials you buy just for this.

All the time you are decorating your key, know that you are doing more than just making it pretty... decorate it with intention, with the intention of enchanting it.

Transform your key into a magical tool for opening the doors to enchantment, opening the way to Faery.

All you really need is attention, but if you like you can mark out a magic circle, light a candle and say a prayer...

---

[4] http://www.catherynnemvalente.com/fairyland/about

Faery folk come gather round,

Bless this key that I have found!

Let it now become enchanted

To open doors where it is planted!

Thread a ribbon through the hole in the top and wear it round your neck when you want to invite more magic in, to remind yourself to be aware of the Fae folk, the kissing of magic and mundane worlds, as you move through your life.

Hang it above the entrance to your home to encourage enchantment to flow in.

Use it to draw doors in the earth outside, to open the way for magic to come through.

Place it before you, light a candle, and muse on the question of what doors you wish to open, and what doors you wish to close in your life. Then hold the key and turn it in each lock as you imagine them before you, one way to open, the other to close. Wear your key as you take steps to help the magic open and close the doors you've asked it to, and sleep with it under your pillow to open the doors of enchantment in your dreams.

May doors open for you and let beauty and delight flow into your life where you most need it.

Spirits of Things   30th January 2011

Hello Feylings!

The key which inspired the key-kiss was a gift to the main character of a story, September, from a coat with a life of its own, and the key itself has its own adventure...

Not only is the key an enchanted creature capable of opening doors, then, it is also revealing something magical about the world we live in. Everything is alive. Everything has a spirit. Everything has a heart.

I'm a natural hoarder, I collect objects and carry them from place to place. Recently I've been thinking, if everything has a spirit, what does the way I treat my belongings show about my relationship to the world? And to spirits and other beings in the world? If I have so many things I cannot give them all the attention they deserve, what does that say about me?

Have you ever really thought about this? How do you treat your belongings? What do they mean to you? Why do you have what you have, buy what you buy, keep what you keep and release what you release?

What would the Western world be like if we acted as though every thing has a spirit?

Could animism of this form be the way to help us connect to the world around us in a healthy way, in a less wasteful way?

When you choose a key to enchant, listen to its heart. What doors will it open for you? How would it choose to be dressed in enchantment? Can you enter into a partnership with your key, to work together in re-enchanting the world?

I intend to slowly transform how I interact with the objects in my home and the world around me into a more conscious, deliberate, loving way of being. To treat things more as beings with a spirit and a life of their own over the next year or so, and to see how this affects my life.

If the whole world is sacred, divine, part of the Great Spirit by whatever name, then how can we live together with all the beings in our lives in a way that reflects this belief?

And, a final thought which would need a much longer exploration... if we return to the book which inspired the post: does it have spirit as a digital book in the same way as the physical books will have once they are held in hands and living on shelves?

Happy thoughts and Pixie Dust,

~Halo x

Pixie Kiss #10: A Faery Adventure

When Spring arrives, or the sun peeks down at you, and you have some time to yourself, go looking for enchantment.

Choose a few hours, or a whole day, which you can set aside for an adventure.

Get your coat and bag (if you'll be taking one) ready before you start. Take cookies.

Before you leave the house, take a moment to sit with your Faery inspiration, the pictures and stories you've collected, the photos you've taken, the altar you built to enchantment. If you've made a Faery key hang it round your neck, or slip it into your pocket.

Imagine what it would be like to be a creature of magic and enchantment, connected to the natural world. Imagine what you'd look like, how you'd feel, how you'd move if you were to express the part of you that is fey.

Let that image, the feeling, settle into your bones. Feel the wings or horns or tail you imagine as though they were there. Feel your body move into that posture, really embody that feeling. Become Fey.

Grab your coat, bag and shoes, or whatever you need, and walk out the door, holding that feeling.

Go for a wander. Get on the first bus you see. Take a random turning that you don't normally walk down. Keep your common sense and watch out for cars or areas where you don't feel safe, and go exploring.

If you choose to, you can set a destination and go to a specific place to explore.

Or you can see where the faery music leads you. Open to inspiration. Listen to the music that rests on the wind. Watch for faery eyes that peer out at you.

Breathe in life and magic and experience the world with the heart of a fey.

Be open to messages and gifts. The world around us speaks in symbols, the world of magic draws near. Watch for the signs of spring, if you live somewhere where they're showing.

Leave an offering of cookies somewhere appropriate for the fey.

Talk to them.

Remember to come home...

If you like, experiment with this process on journeys you already have to take, or in places you are already. Explore your home and see how it feels to Fey-like senses, how much does it encourage enchantment?

How does it feel to be fey?

Spring! 4th February 2011

Hello Feylings!

This week I woke up to see flowers peeking through the soil, and the air outside had an edge of warmth, as though the world knows Spring is coming!

Today it is almost stormy, and this Imbolc I've travelled to Glastonbury, land of apples and enchantment, to celebrate with my community.

On the bus here I played with being open to enchantment, thinking about how we can remain enchanted even when dealing with public transport, and about how it's so easy to go on an adventure. How many cool places are within an hour's travel of your home that you've never gotten around to visiting? I know I've overlooked several gorgeous places near my home in Wales where I'd love to go. This year I'll be making an effort to have mini-adventures, just for an afternoon. Where might you go exploring this year?

Happy adventures this coming spring!

Happy thoughts and Pixie Dust,

~Halo x

Pixie Kiss #11: Seeing Faeries without Sight

I've always looked for faeries, and very rarely seen them.

I often feel them, however, or know that they are near.

It turns out that not everyone can translate their experiences into something visual, and that is ok. This means, however, that in a world which emphasises sight so much, we can overlook our own experiences in the pursuit of a pattern which does not suit us, as I did for a long time.

Always *looking*, rarely *seeing*, but I knew they were there. I knew there was something to see... when I finally gave up on seeing, I found them.

Don't worry, then, if you cannot see them. They are still there.

Scientifically it has been shown that our brains filter out the information which our subconscious has dictated is not necessary for survival. Since we are communal creatures, part of our survival involves not noticing those things that get us into trouble, like faeries, and other beings which our culture tells us do not exist.

Combining the brain's filtering system with our emphasis on sight when not everyone operates in a visual way makes sensing the fae that little bit harder.

Add into that a whole mess of geological and hormonal factors which can affect our ability to sense that which goes beyond the physical and its no real wonder that we miss them.[5]

And yet... the mythological component in our lives is important. Having a good relationship with the world as alive in its own right, rather than as merely something to be used, is important. Connecting with those beings that live beyond the surface of the world is important.

We can reconcile these elements by practicing awareness.

We are more receptive to these energies when we are relaxed and in a playful state of being. The part of our brain which encourages the ability to sense these things is most active in the early hours of the morning. The electrical interference from modern day living is quietest at this time too, and outside in a natural setting. We can open to sensing the Fae using whichever method works best for us – seeing, hearing, feeling, knowing, even smelling... be aware of how you work. Be aware of your surroundings. Be aware of when you feel most open.

Be aware of your self first, and then you can become aware of the Others.

With that in mind I recommend the following process if you would sense the Fae:

Spend some time imagining that you can see and hear faeries. Play a little. Relax.

---

[5] For an interesting and accessible discussion of the science behind the magic I recommend the fascinating book 'The Faery Faith' by Serena Roney-Dougal, including an explanation of why, perhaps, we've lost the ability to sense otherworld beings as easily as we once did.

Go outside, in the early hours of the morning before dawn if possible, to a beautiful place in nature.

Get as far from electrical devices as you can. Switch off your mobile phone and mp3 player, leave the laptop at home.

Breathe deeply.

Relax.

Hold the intention of sensing faeries, and ask, aloud if possible, if this is the right place. If you feel welcome, peaceful, happy, accepted or otherwise positive in response then continue here, otherwise move on and repeat until you find a place where the beings are happy to talk to you.

Allow sensations to arise, impressions relating to whichever senses work for you.

If you struggle, pretend that you are in a fantasy world and that faeries are a part of everyday life for everyone. In reality, this is not far from the truth if you think about the recent past, or other cultures. Remember that many people interact with spirit beings daily, and that you are able to do this too.

Relax, breathe, and allow impressions and sensations to come to you.

When you are ready, thank the space and the beings that came, leave an offering of food or drink, and return home.

Make a note of what you noticed, and watch your dreams.

Clean House

If you choose to have guests round
In good spirits let your house be found
For space to breathe and stretch and flow
Is where the Fairest Folk will go
And if they like it, you will know
As they will come again

Stepping Outside   11th February 2011

Today I walked through the rain.

It was like the world was washing all my cares away.

What I thought was grey sky transformed, as I watched, into fog laid low over the hills.

The rain ran round the rim of my hat, pulled down against the wind-borne drops, and poured past my face to rejoin the rivulets of water flowing past my feet along the road.

And freshened by the rain, washed clean, fed, the land glowed with life. Trees sang happily to themselves in the sound of mist made solid dripping from their leaves.

The natural world is alive. I know it. You know it.

To leave the house, even when everything is soaked through, and to walk amoung the trees... step outside and open to the world... watch the green glow of life as it flows. To connect to the realm which the Fae embody is to feel alive again.

At a recent workshop I took people outside and directed them to connect with the green world, with the trees, to learn about the flow of life. In honesty, the natural world has much more to teach us than this, and listening directly to it, connecting to the Fae who are conscious forces of the natural world , is one of the most healing things we can do.

Happy thoughts and Pixie Dust,

~Halo x

Pixic Kiss #11.5: Valentine's Day

In honour of the modern Festival of Love...

Isn't it lovely to have a day devoted to love? A day set aside specifically for connecting to loved ones, for being romantic?

As I write this, tomorrow is Valentine's day.[6]

Don't forget, you too are worthy of love.

Sometime this week, treat yourself. Take yourself on a date, even if its just an hour to yourself for a candlelit bath, or your favourite warm drink and a cozy armchair.

Living in enchantment means loving life, loving the world, and loving ourselves. Use the week of hearts and flowers to remind yourself that a little luxury is good for the soul... the Faeries know this well, that is why so many of them feast and dance and celebrate whenever the opportunity arises; life is worth a little living!

Happy Love day sweethearts!

---

[6] Even when you read this and Valentine's day isn't drawing near, treating yourself to a date with yourself and showing yourself love is a good way to feel enchanted. I highly recommend this at least once a month! Friday for example, as Freya's day, is a good day for celebrating luxury, love and beauty.

Pixie Kiss #12: Gratitude

To live an enchanted life, we must choose to be enchanted, and we can choose to be enchanted by the positive parts of life.

I have often seen it suggested that a gratitude journal is a good thing to keep, and I agree. To remember the good things, to remember what we are grateful for every day, is to invite more of that into our lives. Holding an attitude of gratitude throughout the day not only lets the universe know that we love the good things it has gifted us with, it also encourages us to see the world in a softer light, with connection and compassion rather than defensiveness and aggression.

Sometimes it feels that we have nothing to be grateful for. At those moments, stopping, taking a breath and just being grateful for the air is enough to shift our relationship with the world at that moment. List those basic things you are grateful for, running water, family, health, people that support us through ill-health, the gift of beauty, the budding flowers, the sparkling snow. This shift of focus in times of struggle helps us to relate to the world in an enchanted way, a way which allows us to feel the wonder inherent in nature.

Choosing to start the day with this attitude sets you up for the day.

The same principle works with other attitudes. Wonder, for example. Choosing to notice the wonderful things in the world, or to approach the day with a sense of wondering, allows for a more playful, joyful, wondrous way of being.

As the day begins, set your intention. If you feel it is appropriate, you can ask the fae to bless your intention and support you in it.

As the day continues, recall this intention and try to hold the feeling you have chosen in your heart.

As the day winds down, muse on the parts of the day that reflect that feeling back to you.

Notice, as time goes by, how these positive feelings help you to react in a way more beneficial to yourself and to the others around you.

Some intentions and attitudes to inspire you to find your own:

Gratitude

Wonder

Inspiration

Delight

Peace

Grace

Ease

Reframing acts and Support   18th February 2011

Hello Feylings!

Today has been the day of the full moon, and I'd like to share a story from this week with you...

On Tuesday I joined Maryann Devine of smArts and Crafts[7] in her Secret Play-Date, where you allow yourself an hour to play creatively, giving yourself the space to think about a problem in a different way.

Since a November I've been toying with the label 'Enchanter' for myself. Well, this Tuesday's playdate gave me a new perspective. I decided to make my work space nice, to help me uncover how to move forward with my Vision. As I was tidying and unpacking and decorating, I came across my Ritual Robes - purple! with a serpent! - and decided that this process of organisation would make a great overtly magical act. On goes incense and robes to accompany my usual Star Goddess Candle!

Creating my space as a magical act reminded me that intention is important in everything we do, and that I can build my Vision as a magical act.

I began musing on the idea of being an enchanter, and I came to realise that my main tool for enchantment is this blog, and words in general.

---

[7] http://smartsandculture.com/blog

It seems, then, that my Craft, as an enchanter, involves writing... and that writing can support me at the same time as I share it with the world! Something I feel very strongly is that we can change the world. Even if, through our attitude and intention, we succeed only in making the world a little more enchanted for one person, then we've made a difference. If we can model an enchanted life in ourselves, then others will be able to see how life could be different, better, more wonderful! This is something I'm working on, offering tools and suggestions for people to help enchant their own selves (as you know) in the hopes that in can brighten the lives of the people who read it, and perhaps that will ripple out from them too...

In order for you to do what you love, and to do what helps others, that work needs to support you. Since our world operates primarily on the energy of money, I need to find ways of offering people methods which they are happy to support me through. I'm struggling a little with this concept, as I'm sure you'll understand, since I'd like to be able to not worry about that side of things at all... and yet, this is life. We have to be aware of the possibilities, of the energies of the world, and of what we need. We have to choose to support ourselves, and let others support us in return for the work we do.

What is it you love? And how can you allow what you love to support you more? This needn't be financial support, although it might be... every passion we have can feed us in return, whether through sheer enjoyment or monetary flow. What are you passionate about, and how does that feed you?

And, don't forget, re-framing a mundane act as a deliberately magical one helped me shift my thinking and come to a decision about where I choose my path to turn, beginning with the full moon today. Is there something you might like to re-frame as a magical act, to help you shift your thinking? Intention and attitude :) good luck!

Thank you for walking beside me as I find my way on this path!

Happy thoughts and Pixie Dust,

~Halo x

Pixie Kiss # 13: Casting a Faery Circle

In many magical traditions, a circle is cast. Circles to protect, circles to contain, circles to focus, circles to mark out a space beyond the everyday world.

Here we will look at circles, not circles that divide us from the world, but circles of blessing and transformation.

Before you begin, leave an offering for the spirits of the place you are in, cookies, milk, chocolate, an apple, a song... leave a gift in honour of those beings that live here, asking if it is ok for you to play here, today.

Breathe.

Relax.

Call to your faery guide, ask them to guide you and support you as you create a circle of blessing. Ask them to ward your space with you if you know how, or for you if you do not.

Imagine the mists that rise from the earth. The Faery mists, rising slowly.

Hear the music in your mind, and allow the sound of tiny bells to surround you.

Feel the sunlight, or moonlight, or starlight, on your skin, kissing the crown of your head.

Breathe in as the mists rise and allow the sunlight or moonlight or starlight to pour in through your crown. The light flows into your heart and out down around your arms, focussed by your hands.

Direct the light into the rising mists and spin slowly, one hand outstretched to let the light flow into a circle around you, the other held near your heart to remind you to let the energy flow with love.

As you turn and the light flows and the mist rises and the circle forms around you, hold in your heart a sense of love, gratitude, blessing.

Once the mists have risen to surround you, and you feel a circle of light and faery blessing around you, stop in the centre and ask your guide if they have any advice for you about this circle.

By its nature this circle will attract positive energies and beings, and the wards your guide sets will repel anything unwelcome.

Spend some time in the circle of blessing, allowing its magic to heal you, comfort you, support you.

When you are ready to leave, stand in the centre and begin to spin the other way, slowly unwinding the magic. The mists will sink into the earth carrying the light and love of the circle into the land in blessing.

Breathe.

Thank your guide and ask them to take the wards down if necessary.

Thank the spirits of the place you are in.

Hold the feeling of blessing in your heart and, if you feel like you have too much energy left over from the circle, allow it to overflow into the world, breathing it out in blessing and healing to go where it is needed most.

Then eat and ground and do something mundane!

This circle can be used for blessing a space, for healing, for protection, to denote a place for a magical working, or simply to invite the Fae into for dancing, though if you choose to dance with the Fae you might want to set yourself an alarm or other reminder to come back!

Cycles   25th February 2011

Hello Feylings!

Its a strange world... last week I wrote 11 posts in a row, this week I've posted only one, on marking out space as sacred, as blessed.

Some times we need to be quiet, some times we need to speak out.

I am breathing this week, and turning inwards, pulling together and shaping up things to bring out into the world when the time is ready... stepping into the circle of blessing and power to hold the space and time I need.

Where are you? Are you following the moon inwards, or the sun outwards?

Where-ever you are on your path, blessings to you!

Happy thoughts,

~Halo x

Pixie Kiss #14: Casting a Glamour of Wonder on the World

"Glamour Bombing" a form of artistic and poetic terrorism that involves acts of random beauty, inspiration, joy, magic or wonder with the purpose to raise ambient levels of glamour in the environment, glamour being the unique magic of the fae.

A glamour bomb is any public act or work that aims to inspire genuine curiosity and childlike befuddlement, a change of thought process, belief in magic, belief in the fae, and/or a sense of wonder in the recipient.

~From the glamourbomb 'Tribe.net'[8]

If you've been following the music for a while, letting these kisses from the pixies enchant you, enchantment should be blossoming in your life... cultivating a sense of wonder is a magical act.

Allowing enchantment into your heart is a good step, but perhaps you feel called to share some of that wonder with the world?

One way to do this is to practice the art of 'glamourbombing'.

Inspired by random acts of kindness[9] and Hakim Bey's poetic terrorism[10], a collection of enchanted individuals decided to bring glamour back to the everyday world, and set out to do so in very concrete ways.

Essentially performance and guerrilla art imbued with magical intent, glamourbombs are acts designed to cause a little dissonance in people's minds, enough to stop them for a

---

[8] http://glamourbomb.tribe.net/

[9] http://en.wikipedia.org/wiki/Random_act_of_kindness

[10] http://sniggle.net/Manifesti/poeticTerrorism.php

moment, and then to inject the idea of the possibility of magic, wonder, the fae, enchantment. From leaving notes scrawled by the fae in books and on walls, to gathering in costume as a collective of trooping fae granting wishes and sharing poetry, glamourbombing tends towards the beautiful and bizarre.

Enchantment shared is a wonderful thing, and gentle actions which inspire wonder and the thought that, perhaps, life can be fun and fantastical, can open others to a little more joy in their lives, even if its only a smile at the courage of others to play. Seeing that other people are capable of feeling the enchantment and sharing in a playful way can be a moment to treasure and remember when that is what your heart calls for.

Lead by example, share the enchantment.

While we're on the subject, you might like to explore what alternatives to the term glamour 'bombing' there might be, since I understand the root of the word to be a surprise act which dismantles the current reality, in this case in favour of magic and wonder, but so much of our world is violent and soaked in war... perhaps we can find alternatives in our language that can shift our thinking into something more about beauty and connection than violence and disconnection...

Any thoughts?

How about... Glamour-gasm?

Musing on Glamour'bombing'   4th March 2011

Hello Feylings!

I've been thinking about 'Glamourbombing', except, as I've mentioned, 'bombing' seems counter-intuitive to the process of enchantment.

The name came from the idea of an explosion of magic, a disruption of normal awareness... but it also implies war, violence and injury.

I'm not interested in injuring others, instead I'd like to support them in finding the magic in their lives, open their hearts and minds to possibilities. This is not done through fear.

This kiss has sparked a discussion about the Warrior archetype and energy, with one person uncomfortable with martial terminology altogether, and another feeling that our culture's perspective of 'warrior' as negative is harmful, leading to passive-aggressive behaviour rather than honest confrontation and courage.

The Warrior is an archetype that is important, that direct, strong, assertive power, that standing tall with courage and being willing to fight for what you believe in is key to many parts of life. And we need not treat life as a confrontation needlessly.

I'm personally of the opinion that, in the context of this project of enchantment, invoking war or fighting based energies is not helpful, though denying them totally is not helpful either. The concept of a peaceful warrior may be helpful here: someone who has the ability and courage to stand firm and act assertively where needful, and who does not pursue needless confrontation or violence. Spread enchantment gently where you can. When you reach walls, then stand firm and take action. We can be more than one thing, an enchanter can be a warrior too.

It is important to hold an awareness of your words, words have power, our words shape our reality. Often our culture talks in terms of violence, and creative people often counteract that by going too far the other way, avoiding all directness in favour of wishy-washy-ness. How can we balance love and caring with direct honesty and action?

What kinds of language would you use?

Happy thoughts and Pixie Dust,

~Halo x

Pixie Kiss #15: A Magic Wand

Faeries, enchanters, magicians, witches... all known to be carriers of the elusive magic wand. Evidently this is an important tool for all those who would choose to spread enchantment in their lives, and the lives of others. In this case, perhaps we should make one ourselves!

The wand represents your will and your voice, it can be used to focus, or to symbolise the world tree which bridges all the worlds and can thus carry you between them. Your wand will fill with enchantment as you use it, and become a reminder for yourself of the magic in the world as well as a charmed object in its own right. One day you'll realise that simply picking up your wand brings more enchantment into the world!

Invite your guide to walk with you, and wear your key.

First, find a newly fallen branch.

It must be fresh, and it must be happy to come with you... if you find it hard to tell, ask your guide and see what response you get. (Literally; ask out loud and see what feeling you get in response).

You can take as long as you like over this, and perhaps, in your wanderings, you'll find branches that have been pruned which are suitable.

Try and identify which tree the branch came from and thank it and the spirits of the place, offerings are always welcome!

Take the branch home and spend some time with it in the Faery Circle described in Pixie Kiss #13.

Would it be happier with or without the bark? With carvings showing the pale wood beneath the bark in patterns, or half and half? Does it want to be painted bright colours, draped in ribbon and decorated with crystals? Or would it prefer fur and feathers? Copper wire in spirals? Silver wire in bands? Pyrography? Bells?

There is no rush. Take your time musing on what says enchantment to you, and what feels like it would suit the branch you've brought home with you.

Then, when you have a good sense of where to start, begin.

Allow the mists to soak into it while you work, allow yourself space to play with materials and patterns. Imagine you are a being of magic, crafting a tool and a companion in the shape of a wand who will walk with you on this path, spreading wonder and enchantment throughout the world!

Take as much time as you need and, when it is finished, sit in the circle with it and listen for its name...

This is the enchanter's main tool, an extension of their Will. Play with your wand often, drawing patterns in the world around you and allowing a sense of wonder and enchantment to flow out into the world like light.

Play with casting the circle of blessing using the wand instead of your hand to direct the flow, or to draw doors in the world which you unlock with your key!

Bless the world with wonder.

Smile at a Stranger
March 2011

Hello Feylings!

A brief thought for today:

If everyone smiled at a stranger today, just one, can you imagine how much happier the world would be? Just from one simple act. If we can bring some happiness to one person's life each day, even if its only one, even if its just a little, then we've done something enchanting.

Enchant someone today, smile at everyone!

Happy thoughts and Pixie Dust,

~Halo   x

Pixie Kiss # 16: The Faery Queen's Blessing

She who goes by many names, who wears so many faces...

The embodiment of Faery itself, The Faery Queen is the consciousness behind the patterns, the weaver of the web that underlies the natural world. Faeryland is the world of the spirit, the world of blueprints from which our world manifests, and she is the one that directs the creation of these blueprints.

Sit for a time in the space you have made for yourself, with the tools you have created, with the stories and artworks you have collected. Ask your guide to be with you, as witness and guardian.

Muse on who you are and why you want to bring more enchantment into your life, into the world.

Cast a circle in the faery mists, a circle of blessing which will move with you, breathe in and allow it to settle around your body and go to a wild place of beauty.

Breathe out and let the circle of mists expand around you. Hold your musings in your mind...

Why do you want to enchant your life, the world?

Stand under the open sky and allow your senses to soften...

Let your heart call out to the Queen of Faery and, perhaps, she will come with the sound of bells or music or the scent of wildflowers to bless your choice to walk the path of enchantment.

Spend some time with her, in honour of her.

Maybe you feel called to make a pledge, maybe you simply feel her kiss on your forehead in blessing.

When you are ready to leave, thank the Queen and your guide, and allow the circle to sink into the earth, blessing the land beneath your feet. Leave an offering for the spirits of the place and return home.

Eat, drink water, do something mundane and get grounded!

Pixie Dust - A Recipe

As every faery lover knows, pixie dust is an essential ingredient of faery magic. In the spirit of play, I encourage you to make some for your own enchantment...

Gather together three or more of these ingredients;
Flower petals, fallen, for colour
Wildflower seeds, for growth
Tiny pieces of quarz, for light
Your favourite enchanting music, for joy
Found feathers, for flight
Sugar, for sweetness
Spices, for excitement
Charms, wood, or other items you feel drawn to include[11]

Take your ingredients and a bowl to a beautiful place, under the full moon or a bright sun, create a circle of blessing and ask the Faery Queen for her guidance and blessing ask you mix your magic powder.

Keep some close by and, whenever you feel the need for a splash of enchantment, sprinkle the powder as a blessing on yourself or the land.

As Peter Pan taught us, Pixie dust plus happy thoughts gives us the gift of flight... Use accordingly.

---

[11] Have a care for the environment if you might use this outside as items like glitter or plastic confetti do not degrade well.

On Offerings

Inviting guests in and then not offering a cuppa is often considered rude when dealing with other humans, and in the same way, the Fae appreciate offerings too.

An offering, whether left outside in their space as a gesture of thanks, or laid out inside as for a guest, can be many things, including:

cookies

cakes

fruit

chocolate

poetry

stories

music

dedicated acts...

Generally speaking, it's nice to share, and something biodegradable which can be left safely outside for them to enjoy is always good, as is something which has emotional investment.

Offerings are a way of showing that you are not just after something, but would like to enter into a relationship based on friendship, respect and trust. It is the same as offering a gift to your host, especially when you've turned up uninvited, to show gratitude, or offering hospitality to people you've invited round.

Fae folk are known for their love of sweet things and beauty, and showing respect for the area you leave the offering in, by making sure it won't leave a mess or cause damage, is a good way of demonstrating that you are a thoughtful human being.

Appendices

Appendix 1: A Creation Story

Long before time was time, the world was born of stardust. The earth, she lived and breathed. Her heart beat. Her soul sang into the universe, singing in chorus with her brothers and sisters, the other planets. The stars, older than she and her siblings, watched and loved, knowing the young planets to be kin.

The heart of the Earth beat. Each beat held a spirit, and each spirit danced between the centre of the Earth, and the realm of the stars. The stars, too, had hearts which beat, and their heartbeats each held a spirit, and these spirits danced with the heartbeats of the Earth, and all were together. These beings, which arose from the heart of the earth and the stars, were the Fey ones.

The Earth began to grow. As she settled into her skin she drew the sky around her like a cloak, and in the warmth between the sky and her skin, the plants grew and oceans settled. From the wombs of her oceans, animals were born, animals which grew and changed. Some grew into feathered beings, some into reptiles, some into furred ones, and some, eventually, into humans.

The Fey were fascinated by the beings birthed from the Earth and they watched carefully as we grew and developed. They guided us, played with us, danced with us through our early years. And we danced with the Fey and all the other beings of the earth and sky and sea.

But over time we found great power, and in our rush to be great, we began to lose sight of the heart of our Mother Earth, we stopped hearing the songs of the Stars. For us, their hearts had stopped beating. And when we stopped hearing the heartbeat of our mother, we stopped seeing how she was alive. And so it became easier for us to use her without giving back, without remembering that we are a part of her. Our power over the land grew great, and in the flush of amazement, we were lost in the maze that led away from gentle wonders, we lost sight of our relationships with the other beings of this world. We went from weak to strong, but we forgot where the spirit that fed our strength lived… we forgot that there is strength in wonder and vulnerability, and we donned our armour of brittle power, and we forgot the ones who had opened our eyes to the possibility of possibility.

And so the spirits of the heart of the stars and the earth became sad. The bright ones, the darks ones, the dancing ones, they drifted back into the heart of the earth, to roam upon the upper lands only in times of celebration or sorrow, to remind us of our kin. But the distance proved too great, and we forgot how to see them, we forgot to listen to the heartbeat of the Faery realms.

The worlds drifted apart. We lived in one world, where all is matter and for us to use. They lived in another, where all is alive and related to each other. And they wept, and we grew in power, but bit by bit forgot the essence of joy.

But, do not despair, for there is more to the tale than this great divide between spirit and matter, magic and material, for every night and day that the Faery host roamed, there would be one who told the tale. For every moment where the worlds became close again, kissing, one with eyes to see and ears to hear might find themselves seeing and hearing the music of the Fey, the enchantment of the heartbeat of the earth. And every time the Fey from the stars descended, we were reminded of the glorious beauty of life beyond the dust of the world we had chosen to walk within. These moments were passed on as stories, stories shared over campfires, at bedtime, in songs.

And the stories begin to weave a web, a picture. Some stories tell of those Fey beings who cause trouble, some of those who help, some of great beauty, and others of great illusion. What we must remember, however, is that each of these stories contains a little truth, and that while the worlds of Fey and Human can sometimes misunderstand each other, always, when each approaches the other with respect, love and an open heart, there is great magic to be found... the magic of the healing of the Earth.

Bridging the worlds of Faery and Human, the light of the Earth and the land of our lives, bringing these two together, relights the fire in our lives. In letting magic kiss the mundane, we invite joy into our lives as once again we learn to hear the heartbeat of the earth and stars. Now we are strong on the land, we can choose to be strong in our vulnerable, open hearts again. Will you weave with me, with the others working and playing to build the bridges again? Will you weave with us the understanding of both worlds? Will you weave together the power on the land with the wonder of the earth's heartbeat, and open to the possibility that to truly know the world, the whole world, is to know the mechanics, *and* to understand the heart?

Originally published in my book *The Faery Heart*, available through **www.haloquin.net**

Appendix 2: A Feyhearted Manifesto

We believe in the wonder of the worlds.

We believe in joy and delight.

We recognise that the world is often full of danger, and that this does not diminish its beauty.

We see feyness in each heart, and are touched by the faeries.

We honour the Wild within and without, and we care for our world.

We pledge to live life as fully as we can.

We choose to share our Delight in the world!

Appendix 3: Other Sources of Enchantment

Goblin Fruit – a delectable online treasure trove of fantastical poetry, make your choices with care as some of the fruit bites back… Find the fruit you should not eat at: www.goblinfruit.net

Oliver Hunter – The artist who adorns Goblin Fruit has some wonderful words and pictures about wonder… when I read his words about 'embroidering everyday life with jeweled colours' and finding enchantment in everyday life I was enthralled. Be enticed at: www.goblinfruit.net/cupfull

Brian Froud – a well known favourite of many, the Fae are known to pose for his paintings, and can easily be seen in his wife's work too! Find the Frouds at: www.worldoffroud.com

Paul Rucker – rich colours, divine inspirations, gods and spirit beings populate his art and his life as he adorns himself with fantasy and steps into the world. All kinds of beauty are in residence at: www.paulruckerart.com

Havi and Selma – Havi writes about getting unstuck, noticing and working on thought patterns and using metaphor to transform 'grown-up' bits of life into playtime. Selma is a duck. Destuckify at: www.fluentself.com

Scarlet Imprint – Actually a publisher, the writings Scarlet Imprint publish are well worth hunting down if you can. Their recent poetry anthology in particular contains some gems of enchantment… Find their writings at: http://scarletimprint.blogspot.com

Victor Anderson – One of the founders of the Feri tradition, along with Cora Anderson, Victor wrote poetry as love songs to the goddess, and she sang back. What better endorsement do you need? Read love letters to the Goddess at: www.lilithslantern.com/victor_writings

Catherynne M Valente – Award winning author of unusual, poetic, prose which transports you and transmutes your world. Discover a new side of the otherworlds at: http://www.catherynnemvalente.com

Maryann Devine – A business coach who knows how to play, and how important enchantment is for creativity and life! Combine business and pleasure at: http://smartsandculture.com/

About the Author

I grew up already enchanted, and at a retreat in early 2009 I rediscovered my connection with the Fey, just under the surface for all this time.

I recommitted to enchantment, with it already in my blood, and began to outline for myself a way of deepening my connection to my own Fey Heart, the beginnings of which can be found within this little book.

My home is in the valleys of Wales, though circumstances may keep me from living there at times. I am a student of the Anderson Feri tradition, a some-time teacher within Reclaiming Witchcraft, an intuitive artist and a creative philosopher, all of which have influenced my path.

I've been practicing The Craft for over a decade, and always, it is true, my heart brings me back to my Queen.

So here I am, and here you are.

I wonder where our paths will take us next?

~Halo Quin

Some of the writings found here were originally published on my blog at www.feyhearted.wordpress.com, where further information about the FeyHearted project and the books still to come may be found.

Other writings, art, and crafts for sale can be found on my website at www.haloquin.net